Recognizing Your

Jesus

in the Flesh

Joy Gill

ISBN 979-8-89345-500-7 (paperback)
ISBN 979-8-89345-501-4 (digital)

Christian Faith Publishing
832 Park Avenue
Meadville, PA 16335
www.christianfaithpublishing.com

Printed in the United States of America

Establishing Intimacy with the Lord

To all my single Christian sisters who are waiting to meet "Mr. Right," I have good news: You already have. Who? Jesus.

Do you not know the moment you gave your life to Christ, the most beautiful love became available to you? Sadly, a few have not learned to bask in the intimate love God desires to bestow upon them. We simply accept His forgiveness of our sins and think that is all there is, but it's not. The Lord does not merely care about forgiving your sins. He cares about you. Jesus wants to have a relationship with you! First Peter 5:7 tells us to cast (bring) all our cares (anxiety) upon Him, for He cares for you. God wants us to come to Him with everything that matters to us.

I want to ask you a question. After giving your life to Jesus, have you moved toward developing an intimate relationship with Him? You might be thinking, *I don't know how*, or *Isn't that only for people in ministry?* No. Every believer is to know the Savior on an intimate level. We are His children. Romans 8 tells us we are joint heirs with Christ.

Therefore, let me ask you again. Since receiving salvation, have you moved toward an intimate relationship with the Lord? Let me walk you through the process. You know how it is when you first meet someone, and although you can't tell them, through engaging in conversation, you think to yourself, *I'd like to get to know this person better.* So you exchange phone numbers, then one of you takes the first step and makes the first call, and in that conversation, you share not heavy-duty things but trivial things about yourselves. That initial call leads to another and another, and then maybe an invite to lunch or an event, and you find yourselves sharing, confiding, and building a relationship that develops into a real friendship. Well, that's how it is in establishing intimacy with Christ. Believe me when I say God wants us to share our cares, hurts, fears, joys, everything with Him, just like you would with your closest friend. He doesn't want us to just come to Him with our complaint of the day or our prayer request, but everything. You may ask, even the things that don't seem important? Yes! When I say everything, I mean everything.

Think of your most intimate earthly relationship. Is it built upon love, trust, and connectedness? Do you find this person easy to talk to and share information with that you would not share with another? That is the kind of relationship Jesus wants to have with you. Just like your relationship with your BFF emerged through spending time and making yourself vulnerable to one another, so will your intimate love with Christ develop. I urge you to spend time sharing your heart, goals, desires, anything you like with Him. Don't be in such a rush when entering His presence. The Bible tells us in Psalm 100:4 (NKJV), "Enter His gates with thanksgiving, and into His courts with praise; be thankful to Him, and bless His name." So the next time you go to God, don't just bring Him your requests. Bring Him yourself. Remember, cords of love create strong bonds. God loves us so hard and wants us to love Him the same.

So what does that have to do with the man of your dreams? Everything! When it comes to love, we are subject to error in judgment without an intimate relationship with Christ. Now this following statement may burst your bubble, but it needs to be said. Just because you go to church does not necessarily mean you have established an intimate relationship with the Lord. Let me repeat by saying it's not the fact that you pray, but what takes place when you pray that makes the difference. Spend quality time with God. Open yourself up to the Holy Spirit and allow Him to touch the very core of you. Allow Him to heal those broken places you have tucked away from the eyes of others. Being intimate is the ability to be raw and naked about what's going on inside of you. You may ask, but doesn't God know? Of course, but He wants to hear it from you.

When we take our innermost thoughts to Him, it shows we are entering a place of trust. Example: Remember how in the formation of your friendship with your BFF, you withheld certain information?

But as time went by and the two of you became close, the story you once regarded as privileged began to be shared. Why? Because trust entered your relationship and fear exited. When a relationship hits its peak, you have moved from chum to confidant. It is at that point that real intimacy begins.

Have you hit that peak with God? Once you do, a whole new dimension in your walk will unfold.

Remember, we're not ready for a genuine relationship until we are ready to share our hearts' secret places. I'm not saying spill your guts to anyone who'll listen. I'm saying that for a relationship to be fruitful, you (in time) must become transparent. Remember this: how well you relate to Christ is a precursor of how well you will connect with your man. Therefore, just as the church is subject to Christ, so let the wives be to their husbands in everything (Ephesians 5:24 NKJV).

Discerning God's Man

Husbands, love your wives, just as Christ also loved the church and gave Himself for her (Ephesians 5:25 NKJV). I used to view this verse as a charge presented to men regarding treating their wives. The Lord knows there are those who need guidance. I'm not saying that to slight the brotherhood. I'm saying this because there are those who honestly do not know how to function in a husband's role. They have not had a role model that they can imitate. That's why the Lord gave them the charge to emulate Him. Notice God did not leave it to the man to take upon himself how to fulfill this charge but gave specific instructions, just as Christ also loved the church and gave Himself for her. Why did God specify how a man was to love his wife? The reason is marriage is the only relationship that physically depicts to the world the love God has for His body, His bride. I once read someone stated, "Husbands and wives are the only panoramic view people see of Christ and His relationship to His church." Therefore, His representatives must represent well.

However, this verse is not just a mandate for men, but it also serves as a cue for the woman. Now you are about to see why it is vital for us to have an established intimate relationship with Christ.

About a year ago, the Lord opened my eyes to something else in the above scripture. Single women who have a relationship with Christ and realize that Christ is their covering and protector can better discern a man who enters her life; therefore, a wife is naturally subject to her husband. So is the single woman to be unto the Lord. Don't live your life rejecting your protection. When we allow the Lord to cover us, we can discern an individual's intent and the Spirit at work by the Holy Spirit. I urge you to ask the Lord to let you see a man through the eyes of the Holy Spirit and not your emotions. As women, we are emotional creatures and are subject to feelings taking us over. The Bible, however, tells us in Romans 8:14 that the Spirit of God should guide us.

Through the eyes of the Spirit, look for the attributes of Christ. Too often, we place more emphasis on spoken words. We can get caught up in how good those sweet nothings (and I do mean nothing) make us feel. However, if you pay attention to how he functions, you will quickly discover his motive, character, and integrity. Remember, the sooner you make your discovery, the better for you. The Lord said that a person's speech would betray them. I remember talking to someone who mentioned how important it is to them to do the right thing. Oh, how they sang! He continued to tell me what he knew about the scriptures and how he once again, "Do the right thing."

Well, during the conversation, I received a package I had ordered. Upon delivery, I discovered I received two of the items I ordered. When I mentioned it to this person, he said for me to check and see if I had been charged twice. So I called my bank and learned the company only debited me for one. I said, "I have to notify the company and tell them what they have done." Well, Mr. "Do the Right Thing" told me to keep it and sell it. At once, I remember my heart sinking. Without him realizing it, his words spoke volumes concerning his integrity. Though not directly, he told me, "Joy, I'm not what you want. I lack the nonnegotiable quality you're looking for, which is integrity."

When someone lacks the essential values, their revelation of lack is my clue to make it a wrap. Remember this: when a woman has an intimate relationship with the Lord, then the Lord is her model of what her man looks like, and when she meets him, her man will imitate how God treats her. In other words, you will see Christ in him. However, if you don't have a personal relationship with Jesus Christ, it will be challenging to recognize Jesus's attributes in another. No one is perfect but God. Don't look for perfection but do wait for who's ideal for you. God has a man. You don't have to step out of character or the Word of God to be with him. It is my personal belief that the one who walks with integrity should stand, and the one who refuses to do so should step.

Love Wisely

When it comes to the affairs of the heart, "Fools rush in where angels fear to tread" is a quote with which I'm certain we all can identify. In other words, we made a life-changing decision with truly little information. Love can be the most beautiful or devastating experience of your life. I want you to experience the former and not the latter. When it comes to love, you want to do what I call "Love wisely." When a person falls in love, two occurrences take place right out of the gate. The first occurrence is the feeling of euphoria or happiness. During this period, you are at an all-time high. Love can have the same effect as that of drugs. Also, just like drugs, the euphoria associated with affection can be short-term. The second occurrence is the state of vulnerability.

From the moment you fall in love, you give that person not only the key to your heart but the power to manipulate it. I'm not saying this to scare nor to discourage you but to enlighten you. Another quote I like is, "Knowledge is power." Don't be naive and assume that because your heart is in the right place, the other person's heart is. Investigate and be observant. In other words, receive what they say but verify. Come off that high that has you looking through rose-colored glasses. I am not saying you do not enjoy the experience, but I am saying have sobriety of mind while you do. A sober-minded person is more discerning than someone intoxicated by blind love.

Therefore, we must be on our p's and q's. No, put down to the sisterhood. We are designed for love. Love and nurture come easy to us. However, our loving nature puts us at risk. Remember, it is not a man's place to reveal to you his deviant intent. That is like asking a burglar, "Please inform me when you intend to break into my home." I'm guessing that will never happen. Please take charge of your well-being and stop putting it in the hands of another. Only a husband is responsible for the protection of your heart, not a Johnny-come-lately. Now take a moment and think about your last failed relationship.

I said for a moment because I don't want you to think too hard and be ready to do a drive-by. Now answer this question. Who was the first to fall in love? I didn't ask who was first to say those three magical words, but who fell in love first. You see, once a person falls in love, they unconsciously surrender power to the other. In other words, if a girl or woman places her heart in the hands of a player, booty caller, controlling, or uncommitted man, she is at considerable risk of laying aside her values and her faith for a boy or man who is not worthy of her. Don't be deceived. When a man genuinely loves you, he will never ask you to compromise or set aside your standard for him. If someone asks you to lose yourself, please lose them instead! You and your values are more important than the selfish, narcissistic requests of anyone.

No one should find themselves doing all the investing while the other makes all the withdrawals. You have two hands. One is for receiving and the other for which we give. If your giving hand is active and your receiving hand is immobile, your relationship is exploitation and not love. When you're doing all the adding while they're subtracting, you might want to consider closing out the relationship's account before it bankrupts your heart as well as your wallet. It is not your obligation to fund a person whose only investment is to drain your life. I don't mean to sound brash, but anyone who doesn't believe enough in themselves to invest in their vision is a low investment for you to place your energy. I heard a man of God say, "Be willing to write a dismissal for the one who brings havoc to your life." We should not only apply this to love relationships but to friendships as well. Who is draining you? Who are your investors? I'm not speaking in financial terms alone."

Who exhausts your emotions? Who wants your listening ear? Scripture says, "And we urge you, brethren, to recognize those who labor among you" (1 Thessalonians 5:12 NKJV). The first step to a more healthy and peaceful life is to purge your life from the three *h*'s, which are haters, hindrances, and hell-raisers. In Matthew 7:18–20, Jesus shows us how to recognize or discern the right people in our lives by what they produce or add to us. Whoever has you crying, praying, and frustrated is not a bearer of good fruit. Now there are times when we all will experience disappointment and hurt feelings in our relationships. Not only will we be involved with these moments, but sometimes we may be the cause of them. However, if someone is doing what I call bringing the neg on the reg, meaning bringing negativity regularly, you may want to reevaluate that relationship.

There is only one way to love wisely, and that is first to learn self-love. The purpose of self-love is not to cause you to feel better about yourself but to enable you to set guardrails that you allow no one to cross. Self-love will also prohibit you from dropping your standards. In other words, self-love is your safety net. You see, practicing self-love allows our value system to kick in. Once this happens, we become more particular and discerning as to whom we authorize access to our lives. Also, self-love motivates us to cherish the women we have evolved into. Anything we admire, we protect. Self-love does not grant entrance to your heart or your body for any man's amusement. If amusement is what he's seeking, tell him to GPS Six Flags, and remind him to take his mask.

Taking Your Rightful Place

Years ago, I preached a message mapping out a husband's and wife's respectful places in the marriage unit. Today, I'm going to speak about a single woman's place in her dating relationship. God's word gives husbands and wives specifications to honor, love, and treat one another with respect. Marriage is the only union that God uses as a representation of His relationship with the church. However, before you get to the altar, you must go through the meeting, building, and establishing a link that will last a lifetime. Since marriage is a higher level of dating, give due diligence to vetting your suitor before marrying him.

The dating stage is where two people get to know one another through spending time together and talking to one another. Oh, how we girls can talk! If we're not talking to them, we're talking about them. Yak! Yak! Yak! The problem is we fail to observe them on a deeper level. We overlook important things like their character, integrity, and relationship with family, friends, and God. How do they look at debt? Do you know their money personality? Do you even know your own, for that matter? If he has children, how often does he see them? You see, too often, we observe such things as the outer appearance, what kind of car he drives, how he dresses, how he smells, and too little attention is given to what will make you cry one day, which is his interior. *Warning*! I'm about to make a statement you might find offensive, but women tend to get more acquainted with the head in a man's pants than the one on his shoulders, and that is (how they say) your bad, not his. Do your homework! Believe me when I say they are doing theirs when it comes to you. We will go deeper into that a little later.

I am not passing judgment, but I am giving sound advice as one who has been there and done that. I have heard it said that when you learn better, you will do better. If this increment of time called dating is not taken advantage of wisely, then you could find yourself accepting a marriage proposal from someone you only know on the surface. Could this be why the word urges us not to fornicate? Sex can be intoxicating, overpowering one's senses. If an undercover lover is not qualified to cover, how can he be from God? Remember, he is to love like Christ, and Christ clothes His bride.

Don't you think you owe it to yourself to know who you're saying yes to honestly? If he's a liar, you're not getting a man you can trust. If he's a deadbeat dad, then you're getting low father material for any future children you may have with him. If a man can't properly love what he has procreated, how can he rightly adore you? I urge you to open your eyes and see your man for who he truly is and not who you've convinced yourself he is. Ask the Lord to let you know this man as God sees him. You may lie to yourself, but God won't lie to you. He will show you the truth about your Romeo. Ephesians 5:6–7 (NKJV): "Let no one deceive you with empty words, for because of these things, the wrath of God comes upon the sons of disobedience. Therefore, do not be partakers with them." Be wise about who you choose to date. Learn to watch your back and not just lay on it. Remember this: it is okay to permit yourself to give them a big fat *no*.

Beware of Predators

As in the animal kingdom, so it is among humankind. There will be predators whose only way of survival is to feed off their prey. Also, just like in the animal kingdom, the act of predation can kill the victim. If you haven't, ask God to help you discern the people who enter your life. Matthew 7:20 says, "Wherefore by their fruits ye shall know them." I'm a firm believer that nothing just happens. I also believe we should be aware of who we give access to our lives and our hearts.

"Keep your heart with all diligence, for out of it spring the issues of life" (Proverbs 4:23).

The Wolf

When a young lady or woman is too available and needy, a guy will consider her thirsty. Hungry wolves view eager women as easy prey. They are naive and easily manipulated. Since wolves look for someone to devour, Ms. Thirsty is a perfect catch. If you are thirsty, quench your thirst in something other than a man. When a man doesn't invest in his own life, he can't value the investment you've made in yours. Therefore, look for the value he has placed upon his own life before comfortably moving him into your world.

I've heard women say, "I want a real man, but I can't find one." First, you are not to find him, but he is to see you. Second, you must become what you hope to attract. As I said earlier, thirsty women attract hungry wolves. Get it? Ms. Thirsty is so longing for love, attention, and acceptance that she makes no demands. She makes no waves because she doesn't want to lose her wolf. She shrinks back and allows herself to be walked over to keep her wolf. She takes care of his needs while her own needs go unmet. She works for him and provides for him. She does anything and everything to get affection and accolades from her Mr. Nobody, and that's just the way her wolf would have it.

Ladies, from the moment you meet a wolf, he sizes you up. His conversation is not to get to know you; it is to discover your weaknesses and vulnerabilities. If he detects you're emotionally healthy (not thirsty), you won't hear from him again. You have no propensity for him to capitalize on. Remember, a hungry wolf is ready to slay and eat, not work. Wolves are unemployed by choice and don't want to work hard at anything, including deceiving you. Also, question a man who wants a relationship without a job. I'm not referring to the retired or physically or mentally impaired. I am, however, speaking about the outright lazy. Relationships require money. The unemployed should not make debts when he's cutting no checks.

The Vulture

Predators who take advantage of someone in an awful situation are known as vultures. They are never satisfied. They tend always to want. Like the bird, a man who possesses the spirit of a vulture can spot his prey from miles away. He searches out the weak, needy, and the broken. He zooms in on the anxiety. Philippians 4:6 (NKJV): "Be anxious for nothing, but in everything by prayer and supplication, with thanksgiving, let your requests be known to God."

Ladies, take it from me; you want to know who you are and whose you are before entering a relationship. If you are not faithful to God and yourself, you will ditch both for the vulture circling you. Notice how the scripture above speaks about not being anxious. Anxiousness has caused people, including yours truly, to make poor and hasty decisions. When you feel pressured or rushed into a relationship, you must inquire why. However, a woman who is broken will be flattered by what she should find repulsive.

Remember, when it comes to matters of the heart, a man/woman will tell you what they want you to know, but God will show you what you need to know. Therefore, after hearing their truth, seek the Lord for the facts! The Lord orders the steps of a good man, and He delights in His way (Psalm 37:23).

The Representative

Ever notice how people first meet everyone (including you and me) and present to others the best side of ourselves? We talk about our strengths and share all our attributes (the real and the decorated). Well, it's the decor I want to expound on. While most mean no harm, others are *bald-faced liars*. They are on a mission to deceive, and they know their true self can't get the job done. Therefore, they create a facade or false identity to represent them. Like the wolf, the representative will engage you in conversation to discover what type of man he must make. For example, whenever I meet a guy and they learn I'm a pastor, immediately they start quoting scripture (if he knows any) or mention how he grew up in the church. Get it? What's important to you is what his representative becomes.

I serve as a child advocate for neglected and abused children. I must look out for the best interest of the child in the judiciary system. Well, just as I labor for a child's best interest, that's what the representative of your Mr. Wonderful does. He looks out for the benefit of your devil by pretending to possess the characteristics vital to you. Have you ever dated or married someone who, in the beginning, was so caring and fun and enjoyable, and then later turned into somebody you felt you didn't know? That's because you didn't. This new person is the *true* man you joined yourself to, and his representative is whom you fell in love with.

Representatives are on the scene long enough to woo and win you over. Once the mission is accomplished, then the real man takes center stage. Therefore, being unaware she fell for a representative, the woman prays and does things to try to get the man they fell in love with back. Here's the problem: that person never existed. He was your devil's advocate. You fell in love with a carefully concocted character of what you wanted in a man. Have you ever been asked, "So what are you looking for in a man?" They need the information to create the counterfeit. Now don't get me wrong; there are guys who genuinely want to know you for all the right reasons. However, it is crucial to be on the lookout for the deceiver. Listen to your gut. Too often, we get the *warning* signal but ignore and push past it. A warning signal is a protection signal. "But ye have an unction from the Holy One, and ye know all things" (1 John 2:20). Pay attention to your warning, or you'll wish you did.

Opportunist Calling

When you hear the word opportunity, what comes to mind? A chance or condition for attaining something good, right? Well, an opportunist is a person who looks for someone they consider suitable to use. They prey on someone they can manipulate and use for their selfish agenda. Be it sex, money, or whatever, the opportunist will capitalize and mooch off the labor of others.

The opportunist is a burglar lurking in the shadows, waiting to steal the heart of his latest victim. For he knows the winning of her heart is the key to a successful robbery. This thief goes undetected because the stolen possessions are what the owner gave him access to, which is the entry into her heart. I remember watching this program, and the topic was relationships. I can't remember if the host or guest made the statement, but I'll never forget what he said: "Whoever is the first to fall in love makes themselves vulnerable to the other." Therefore, it's imperative to learn who you're dealing with, so take your time.

Remember the wolf? Like the wolf, the opportunist will examine his prey for weakness through visual and hearing cues, and boy, do we chatterboxes give off the signals. Learn to zip your zipper. In James 1:19, we're encouraged to be swift to listen and slow to speak. Sisters, do it the Bible way. There is safety in doing so. For starters, you'll learn to collect information instead of gathering little to none. Pay attention. Don't get so caught up in getting the care that you don't pay attention.

Not just that, but your conversation isn't a conversation but more of an interrogation. He is doing all the fact-finding while you're spilling your guts.

Have you ever noticed that once you start asking your questions, their replies are vague, or do they avoid answering? Or how about this one? "I don't want to talk about me right now. I just want to get to know you." If so, how did you respond? My response is, "Don't ask me a question you don't want to answer yourself." If a guy wants to know you for all the right reasons, he will also want you to know about him. While you may find talking about yourself flattering, learning about him will prove more rewarding; as I said earlier, an opportunist, like a predator, searches for weakness within his prey. Therefore, converse from a stance of dialogue and not monologue. Remember, the opportunist comes equipped with tactics. Likewise, you should have an arsenal of tools to counteract his tactics. Use your head, and do not lose your heart. Be the prize and not the quest.

The Narcissist

One of the most toxic and unhealthiest relationships one can be involved in is a relationship with a narcissist. Before going any further, let's define what a narcissist is. A narcissist is a person who has a personality disorder known as narcissistic personality disorder (NPD). Studies show that 1 percent of the general population suffers from this disorder. People who suffer from this disorder have an extreme sense of entitlement. They are self-centered and unable to maintain close relationships due to noticeable symptoms such as arrogance and superiority. They desire power over their significant other. Their disrespect and disregard for others can be a result of low self-esteem.

Dating a narcissist is not only a waste of time but can be hazardous to your emotional and physical health. The reason being, these people are incapable of giving genuine love. To the woman who blindly believes her love can change her lover, I say, *"No, it won't!"* The only person who will change in such a relationship is you. Since the narcissist must be the star of a relationship, they will not quit until they reduce you to nothing. Just like the wolf, vulture, and representative, the narc selects his victim. I'll go out on a limb and say the only man who doesn't choose you is God's man. God's man finds you. He discovers who he's called to cover. What's the difference? The man who chooses you selected you for a reason and purpose, not always admirable. The narcissist chose you based on his belief you would fulfill his selfish, egotistical need. For a narc, you are nothing more than a supply filler.

So how do you identify a narcissist? Well, there's no hideous facial appearance if that's what you want to know. They can be charming and quite intelligent. I remember my first and only encounter with a narcissist. He was, as I said, charming, smart, handsome, and a good dresser. Oh, yes, this sister thought she struck gold. When we met, we would talk for hours and laugh and just enjoy each other's company. Then it happened. After a week, out of nowhere, I got my first insult hurled at me. I wasn't certain if he was joking or what. However, when he kept repeating it, I lashed back at him, to which he didn't speak to me for two days. Afterward, he called and at first accused me of insulting him. Not only that, but he also expected an apology. After I reminded him how it started in the first place, he apologized. We decided to start over and did well for a while. However, after a couple of months, it happened again, and not only that, but he also started trying, and I stress *trying*, to tell me what I should and shouldn't do.

He suggested I not wear makeup, jewelry, or heels. He went as far as to say to me I should change my faith. Really? He tried to separate me from my family and friends. Not all, just the ones who intimidated him.

How does the narcissist choose his prey? Since the ego is everything, the narcissist wants women they find attractive, independent, and accomplished. However, his goal is to bring her down to nothing. He needs to shatter her confidence. Making her feel small makes him feel larger than life. Also, the narcissist plans everything. It's as if he lives by a script. I remember one Christmas Eve, my son called to invite my narcissist to Christmas dinner. When I gave him the phone, he did not want to take the call. However, the following day, Christmas Day, he asked to call my son and daughter-in-law. I asked, "What is going on? You wouldn't take his call last night, and now you want to talk to them?" His reply was, "I planned on calling them today." Get what I mean by script?

Also, a narcissist will rekindle the charm if you say you want to leave the relationship. Don't fall for it; keep stepping. As I said, they are incapable of giving genuine love, and the longer you stay, the more in danger you could find yourself. To my Christian sister, marrying a narcissist is like marrying the spawn of Satan. Narcissists never take responsibility for their wrongs, making it impossible for them to have a repentant spirit. The only thing he will possess is you.

Once you no longer fulfill his needs or begin to stand up to him, he will cut you off without notice. He also will return out of nowhere. However, as I stated earlier, it was all scripted. To those of you who are empaths, you're his favorite type. Empaths, please learn to set boundaries. To those with low self-esteem, *boom*! He struck gold. I urge you to learn to love yourself and never settle. Stop lying to yourself. Anytime we decide to be satisfied with less, we lack self-love.

The Weed

Easily detected yet taken home, the weed is a person who for whatever reason chooses to survive off the resources of another. Weeds are charming and charismatic. They can lift spirits and be the life of a party. Like weeds in plant life, these people look like flowers and intentionally position themselves in the life of a flower to live off the nutrients of that flower. On the surface, they look good together, but underneath the soil, the weed drains the life and nutrients of the flower until the flower dies. Are you a flower joined to a weed? Have you been or currently in a relationship where your partner is taking and pulling from you? Do you feel emotionally, mentally, physically, and financially drained? Do they fail to operate in the law of reciprocity? Then, my dear, you are joined to a weed. Weeds are distractions sent by the enemy of our soul to drain the life out of us so that we cannot fulfill our God-given purpose nor richly enjoy our lives. So why do we allow these folks to remain in our lives knowing they drain and suck life out of us? One word keeps women stuck. What is it? Potential. We see what a person can become and make unwise and unhealthy investments that may or may not yield a return.

My oldest son and I were talking about potential, and I like the definition of the word. He said, "*Potential* is one person making a promise to rise and the other believing in the promise, which keeps them tied to each other for years with no fruit coming forth." Is that you? I hope not. Stop investing in people who do not invest in themselves. If anything, you come alongside and invest in what they have started. It is not your job to build their life. Stop confusing Build-A-Bear with Build-A-Man.

The Taken

Are you or someone you know trapped in the mine, yours, and our relationship? In other words, are you hooked by the taken? Is your man still legally married? Although this relationship should be an easy decision, women find themselves believing a guy who says he's leaving his wife for her. According to marriage counselor Frank Pittman, men who divorce and marry their paramours have a divorce rate as high as 75 percent. Statistics also show that 15 percent of men who are financially dependent on their partner are more likely to cheat. A match made in heaven, huh? Ladies, don't fall for the embellished lies. Stop allowing men, as I heard a coach say, "Impregnate your ears." Sisters, in case no one ever told you before, we are the hearing-impaired species. A man's words can catapult us from common sense to nonsense in record time. I have a question for you who are in such a relationship. Ready? Why borrow it when you can own it? If he's married, he's on lease. Meaning, you're living in uncertainty (as well as sin) while he reaps the benefits at the expense of your heart, soul, and reputation. How is that love, sweetie? I have one for you. How about learning to love yourself by gifting yourself with character and integrity that says, "I'm better than what you're offering and, you're not good enough for what I carry"?

The Bible tells us that love works no ill to his neighbor. Therefore, love is the fulfillment of the law (Romans 13:10). This man has no respect for you, nor his wife. Want to know why? Because he has no love for himself. Don't get it twisted; esteem issues aren't a woman thing; it is a human thing. Anyone with unresolved problems or broken places in their inner being requires healing.

To be broken is like a vase that can't hold water. It doesn't matter how beautiful the container is. Suppose it leaks. It is no longer serviceable. Broken humans are like that beautiful vase, and unless we are made whole, our true beauty can't shine through. Your man might not be bad, but he is a broken person behaving inappropriately. Here's something to consider. Humor me, okay? Say you and this guy were to get married, how could you ever trust him, seeing the foundation of your relationship is lies and deceit? You might not believe it, but you will always be looking around the corner to see if karma is coming to visit you. Is that any way to live out your life? Better yet, is that the life you want to live? One more thing, this man will not be able to trust you either. See, you were not innocent in this affair. The man, haunted by his lack of integrity and character, will display bouts of jealousy. I know you are an adult and will do what you want, but my advice is to repent and leave that unfruitful relationship.

Soul Tie

When you hear the term soul tie, what comes to mind? For me, it is an unhealthy and toxic relationship that seems challenging to leave. Sound familiar? If you are or have been in a soul tie relationship, you are not alone. You also can be set free. Let's delve into how and why soul ties originate. The most common is through sexual relations. Sexual relations pave the way for a spiritual connection. Whenever ungodly sexual intercourse takes place (fornication), an invisible tie will develop between the two souls. Since women are prone to connect more quickly than our male counterparts, we can assume the connection we experience is a heart connection on both ends. This thought could not be further from the truth. While there are exceptions to the rule, a night of sex does not generate an investment of the heart.

Once a heart has been captured, it can be challenging to free oneself. The reason being, the one who falls in love first becomes vulnerable to the other. If the other person is insincere, their manufactured lies create a false reality within the mind. When this takes place, the tie gets more robust, and the grip gets tighter. A soul tie relationship is hell-conceived and designed to keep us from receiving the blessing God has for us. It also can hinder or detour us from God's purpose for our lives and ministries. Therefore, let me repeat an earlier statement: find your life purpose before finding your partner.

There are steps to freedom, but know this: it won't happen overnight, and you must be patient with the process.

Step 1: You must pray, pray, and did I say pray? Remember my incident with the narcissist? I had to pray consistently to have that bond broken. If you or someone you know has a soul tie, one of the best prayers you can pray is for God to allow you to see the person and the relationship through the lens of truth. Why? Because you bought into lies, it will take the truth to help break free mentally. Also, ask the Lord to cut the ties at the core of your soul.

Step 2: Forgive yourself. You cannot break free from the grips of a toxic relationship by blaming yourself. While it is essential to see where you were when entering the association—which means what was going on in your life at that time, whether you were in a dark place or on the rebound—it is equally important not to put yourself down nor carry your baggage of guilt.

You might not see it now, but this, too, will pass. You also will be stronger for it. You will discover that God can use it to bring healing, warning, and foresight to others. Remember, Romans 8:28 says, "And we know that all things work together for good to them that love God, to them who are the called according to his purpose."

How to Catch the Eye of Your Jesus in the Flesh

So how do you attract God's man? You must be attractively dressed. I'm not talking about your Prada or your Apple Bottoms but the attitude of your heart. How are you covered? Are you adorned with kindness and sweetness? Or are you bitter, mean, and untrusting? Is your attitude, "This is who I am, take it or leave it"? If so, it could be why they left it. Never expect one person to pay the price for the wrong of another. Never look to anyone other than God to fix what's broken in you.

I'm all for being a strong woman; however, being healthy is strength to the best of its essence. You're not mean, critical, or belligerent. To be healthy is to be able to rock your world while you wait on God. Being healthy is to get your finances in order instead of waiting for a man to come and clear your debt. Being healthy is to walk in your purpose and not sit around talking to other bitter women about who did you wrong or broke your heart. It's the ability to own your part and learn from it. It also means you can walk away from any relationship that is not good for you. Stop embracing the nasty attitude, which is just fear. Learn to be strong in the Lord and the power of His might. Now let me ask, do you need a wardrobe upgrade?

In Matthew 22, Jesus gave the parable about a king who prepared a wedding for his son. Verses 11–12 state, "But when the king came in to see the guests, he saw a man there who was not wearing a wedding garment. So, he said to him, 'Friend, how did you come here without a wedding garment?'"

If we aren't prepared for our moment, then our moment can pass by. The Bible tells us in Proverbs 31 how a virtuous woman is clothed. She's thoroughly together for her position as wife, mother, and businessperson. In so being, she is referred to as blessed. In other words, her family is proud of her. What attire are you wearing? Are you dressed for the occasion? Or do you expect the event to clothe you? You might ask what difference it makes. If missing an opportunity or your blessing is not important, then none. However, if you want to receive all God has for you, it makes all the world's difference. When was the last time you went to a job interview dressed in a bathing suit? Unless you applied for a lifeguard, I would say never. I'm sure you went dressed for success, right? Well, the same principle applies: if you want a good, strong, and godly man, wear godliness, confidence, kindness, love, and a good sense of humor, and you're on your way. In other words, you must be in alignment. Are you in alignment with God's word? A godly man is not seeking a woman who's not correctly aligned. No man wants a negative or victimized spirit controlling the woman he chooses for a wife.

I'm not making light of anyone's hurt or pain. I, like you, have been deeply hurt in my life. However, I decided not to allow Satan to win. What do I mean? You see, pain will accomplish one of two things. It will either (1) hold you captive, filling your heart with poison, or (2) lead you into a soul-searching experience that will carry you into self-discovery and healing. Besides, I had to discover that I was not correctly aligned, placing me in a vulnerable position, which I'll touch on later. However, I made up my mind not to allow the disappointments of life nor the people who played a part in them to hold me in emotional captivity. I refuse to give power over my life to anything but God. Nor can I allow what I've been through to hinder me from being who I truly am: a loving, caring, and crazy (in the comical sense) woman. If you're not cautious, adverse events can alter your personality. Remember, they were events, mere segments of a story God entrusted you to walk out. They can't destroy you unless you allow them. I love life and thank God for everything I've gone through. I'm even grateful for those who were enemies. Why? Because I've come to understand, my enemies have been the only ones who ignited my passion, which fired me up, propelling me into purpose. Through the conduit of pain, purpose is revealed. However, only by the redirection of anger will your goal get fulfilled.

That's why the Bible doesn't say we're not to get angry, but it does warn us not to sin. You and I will never bombard the gates of hell without anger. Without proper outrage, we will allow Satan to walk all over us, destroy our families, and accomplish anything else he sets out to do. So, girlfriends, understand who you are, where you are, and where you want to go. Dress accordingly. Put on the garment of praise for the spirit of heaviness (Isaiah 61:3 NKJV). Remember, a whole man will only take note of and pursue a complete woman. Jesus said it like this: "Those who are whole do not need a physician, but those who are sick" (Luke 5:31 NKJV). A man who has prayed for a wife is looking for his good thing.

Stop looking for a relationship to fix you, and allow Christ to heal you. Anything repaired can be broken again, whereas anything whole won't permit itself to be shattered by anyone ever again. I heard Bishop T. D. Jakes state, "You know you are complete when the patient has become the nurse." Amen! I also want to add you will know you are whole by the type of men you attract. I don't care what you want. You will attract what you are. Why? Because like spirits agree. Do you find yourself drawn to, or shall I say, attracting the same type of guy? Ever wondered why? No doubt, the spirit in you to fix is drawn to the spirit to manipulate your kindness. Know this: dogs will stop sniffing, wolves will cease howling, vultures will no longer circle, and the representative will never fool you once you are no longer the wounded prey.

So what does it mean to understand who you are? When I speak of who you are, I'm talking about who you are in God. Sadly, we go through the motions of trying to be what others want them to be or what they think they should be, not realizing God has a plan. Jeremiah 1:5 (NKJV) says, "Before I formed you in the womb, I knew you; before you were born, I sanctified you; I ordained you a prophet to the nations." Here, God declared to Jeremiah his purpose. If you don't know God's plan, someone will label you and manipulate you into serving their purpose. Often, their mission is less than God's plan.

Let's talk about identity. According to *Webster's Dictionary*, it is "the distinguishing character or personality of an individual: the qualities and beliefs that make a particular person or group different from others." Do you not know that when God made you, he made you in his likeness and image and created, fashioned, and designed you for a unique plan?

We are dictated to by the world how we should look and what size we should be. If we are not careful, we will find ourselves trying to appease society instead of pleasing God.

I'm going to get intimate and share something that will shed light on what I just said. My childhood years were painful for me. I remember always being asked the question, "Are you black or white?" The African American kids had a problem with me because my skin wasn't dark enough, while Caucasian kids had a problem with me because they knew my ethnicity was black. My early childhood years were full of struggle. I was either struggling with the shame I felt over being different or wrestled with the urge not to beat up someone. If you're wondering, did I beat up anyone? Well, let's say I had a couple of suspensions, and oh yes, this sister won! I'm not bragging; I'm just saying. You might ask, did the teasing stop? Not a moment before a shift took place within me. What stopped was my response to foolishness. I came to realize that my most significant hurt wasn't coming from the ignorance of others. It was coming from me. The moment you and I allow others to tell us our value, we've done ourselves enormous harm. When I judged myself by the standard of others, *I* became my worst critic.

Moving forward, four years after receiving Christ, I found myself praying and crying out to God because, once again, I had to deal with the same ignorance of the past within the church. I think, and it is just my opinion, we ought to pray to be set free from the disregard of others. Anyway, I asked God the question, "Why did you make me like this?" Let me tell you, if you have a question, God has your answer. Well, the next night, I went to a revival service where I knew no one, and no one knew me but the friend who accompanied me. We got there a little late, but before the man of God had begun preaching. During his sermon, he said, "I have to change the order of the service." He stepped down from the pulpit and walked down the aisle to where I was sitting, which was an aisle seat. He placed his hand on my shoulder and asked, "Who is Joy?" I replied, "I am." He then said, "The Lord said, 'I have made thee as thou art made that I might use you for my glory.'" He went on to say, "Thou art a prophetess and wilt prophesy to the body of Christ." The Lord has since given me a powerful anointing and has opened His word to me in depths I never imagined. I say this humbly because I'm trying to show you that God has a beautiful plan for your life, no matter what you think or what others think about you.

Now let's get back to identity. The enemy of our soul loves to attack our character. Why? He knows that is where God's plan abides. I believe the root cause of our young people engaging in risky behavior, such as unprotected sex, drugs, and gangs, is the failure of knowing the destiny that awaits them. Unless you are aware of your purpose, you will be a lesser version of your true self. You become a product of your present environment. The present is an increment of time when you prepare for the next space of time called the future. Unfortunately, there are those who remain stuck in a place of learning, never moving toward graduation. Let no man tell you your value. God knows your worth because He alone purchased you with the precious blood of Jesus! Therefore, I urge you not to allow no man to reduce your market value. If he can't afford you, then he's not for you. I heard a man of God say, "Wrong relationships will sabotage your destiny." Yet for whatever reason, young girls and women alike tend to gravitate toward these types of guys. Why? One reason is we as women tend to play Savior to men who are vultures. We allow our motherly nature to kick in. You see, it comes naturally to us to nurture because God equipped us with the ability to be nurturers. The problem is we use the anointing given for motherhood on a man who manipulates our God-given gift. Listen up. God called you to raise your son and not your man. If you're raising him, you're doing it for someone else. Therefore, stop playing Savior and introduce him to the Savior!

Ladies, if you want to catch the eye of God's man, you must realize who you are. Do not allow anyone to change you from who God created you to be. Once you remove yourself from the identity God gave you, you become unrecognizable to the man God has anointed and appointed for you. God fashioned and designed you to fit your husband's needs as well as he will match yours. Everything about you will be perfect for him because your man will see you through the eyes of God. This joke says when Adam saw Eve, he said, "*Woah*, man," and that's how we got the title woman. Well, if that joke carries any truth, you can see that Adam saw through the eyes of God. You never read where he said, "God, you need to change this or fix that." I know we all have something we wish we could change concerning our bodies. It's a woman thing. So whatever you can improve and choose to do so, go ahead. Know this, though, the item you're criticizing, someone else may find attractive. Therefore, improve what you can, and what you can't; stop sweating. Now if you just feel the need to turn yourself into a project, here's something you can do. Work on that attitude adjustment. Get an implant of a meek and humble spirit. Humility is not a weakness.

Don't get it twisted. You can be sweet and powerful. You can be meek, yet nobody's fool. However, no man wants to come home to a hell-raiser. Ask God to prepare you for your husband. Just because you want one doesn't mean you're ready. Ask God for a wife, anointing. You just do things better once anointed for the task. You may have emotional wounds that require healing. Others have daddy issues, and others suffer from trust issues. You have no control over who dropped you, violated you, misused, and abused you, but you can take your power back in the name of Jesus and not allow the actions of others to dictate your behavior toward others. You must first heal from hurts and issues from your past. Marriage is a relationship for the heart's health. Therefore, take time to get the healing you need and deserve, and vice versa. A woman should not consider marrying a man who is not relationship-ready. I once read something that goes like this: "To my future husband, find God. Find yourself, and then find me." Remember, relationships are like a puzzle. If a piece is missing, then it is not complete.

Difference between Good Men and Godly Men

Every woman desires a healthy and secure relationship built with a man who loves them wholeheartedly and unconditionally. However, opinions differ as to what that man looks like. Based on beliefs, biases, attraction, and personal preferences, every woman has a picture of her ideal mate. A godly woman will prefer a man who loves and serves the Lord, whereas a worldly woman won't have that on her list of must-haves. However, all desire excellent quality men. First, let me say, whatever you hope to attract, make sure you are. No one has the right to build their status off another's arduous work. In other words, you are too lazy to get an education but want an educated man. Really? Question: why should you get more and he settle for less? Become what you desire because you will attract what you are.

While having good looks will get a man's attention, a man of substance will quickly lose interest due to your lack of essence. As stated earlier, you must dress for success. In other words, you must be suitable and not just have things in common. To be appropriate means you are right and fitting for them and their purpose. You also need to make sure the man in your life is proper for your assignment as well. Now let us take a closer look at godly men versus good men.

Godly versus Good

So what exactly is the difference between godly and good? Don't they both include morals and values? My answer is yes and no. While both have morals, a holy man seeks to please God. He desires to live by the word of the Lord.

On the other hand, a good man will live under what is right in his sight. Therefore, not all his standards will be in alignment with the word of God. For example, when it comes to purity, a good man may see nothing wrong with sleeping with you before marriage, whereas a godly man will deny the urges of the flesh to obey the word of the Lord. Let us look at the things we as women think of when we speak of a good man. One of the things women look at is the ability to provide. So when you think of a provider, what comes to mind? Money, money, and did I say money, right? I hate to burst your bubble, but if you think all it takes is money for a man to be a provider, you are so wrong and, might I add, shallow. Do not get me wrong. Finances are important. However, being equipped to supply emotional and spiritual security is of immense importance also. Another difference between a good man and a godly one is a good man may sweep you off your feet. However, a God-fearing man won't drop you on your butt. Ouch!

Concluding Thoughts

If you're in a relationship where you are leading and instructing a man, honey, that is not your man. If anything, you are preparing him for someone else. Husband material does not function like a child in need of being raised. That does not mean there won't be things you will not have to enlighten one another on. However, you should never have to raise him like your son. According to Proverbs 22:15, "Foolishness is bound in the heart of a child." A man operating with the heart of a child is not leadership material. Also, any man lacking maturity will possess a shortage of morals, character, and integrity. Not only that, how can you, as a woman, respect such a man? You cannot honor and respect what you have raised. You can only commend yourself on a job well done. Also, all resources invested in a going-nowhere relationship will leave you drained, angry, and in need of healing.

Ladies, until you embrace a loving relationship with yourself (not narcissistic), you will go from one toxic relationship to another. I heard someone say, "Don't want to settle down so bad that you settle." Marriage is the cherry on top of the sundae, not the sundae. In other words, anything you didn't come into the world with, you don't necessarily need to live a happy and successful life. You came into this world with you. Therefore, get to truly know and love you so you can discern who is fit for you. The Bible says, "Seek ye first the kingdom of God and his righteousness; and all these things shall be added unto you" (Matthew 6:33). I encourage you to find God, yourself, and your purpose so that you might know who belongs in your world. We cannot always help who is in our lives, but we must be careful as to who enters our world. What do I mean? Our world consists of those who should share our values, those who strengthen our weaknesses, add to our strengths, and help keep us grounded. I encourage you to wait on God and rock your best life while you wait. Take back the life God gave you and no longer allow another to take it from you. Remember, if they are not adding and multiplying, then they are subtracting and dividing. If they are not respecting you, then they don't love you. Love is not words but action. I passionately believe when a person's love is real, the recipient should be thanking the giver for loving them. If the receiver cannot find a reason to say thank you, then the giver might not be loving correctly. If you're hearing the words but seeing little to no action, you are dealing with a boy and not a man. Boys can only talk what a real man can walk.

My prayer is that each one of you knows you are fearfully and wonderfully made by God and that your value of life is not contingent upon marriage but upon you rocking you. So blow yourself a kiss and adjust your crown, queen. Remember, when you stop settling for paupers, your king will find you.

About the Author

Joy Gill, an ordained minister and board-certified life coach, has over thirty years of experience in helping women in the areas of inner healing and spiritual growth. As a product of divorced parents, she fully understands the struggles and challenges facing women who carry a father's wound. Joy's authenticity and straightforward approach, coupled with her love for humanity, has helped her to reach and teach young women to respect themselves and rise from their past experiences to become the women God created them to be.